Yummy Bites

Creative Lunches for Kids

While every precaution has been taken in the preparation of this book, the publisher assumes no responsibility for errors or omissions, or for damages resulting from the use of the information contained herein.

YUMMY BITES

First edition. March 4, 2024.

ISBN: 979-8224741540

Written by Jose Maria.

Table of Contents

Jose Maria

❖ Introduction

A. Importance of Nutritious Lunches for Children:

Nutritious lunches play a vital role in a child's growth and development, providing them with the energy and nutrients needed to thrive throughout the day.

A balanced lunch supports brain function, concentration, and overall academic performance.

It also promotes healthy eating habits from a young age, reducing the risk of obesity and chronic diseases later in life.

B. Making Lunchtime Fun and Exciting:

Incorporating creativity into lunch boxes can make mealtime more enjoyable for children.

Fun shapes, colorful presentations, and engaging themes can entice picky eaters and encourage them to try new foods.

By involving children in meal planning and preparation, they develop a sense of ownership and excitement about their lunches.

C. Tips for Packing a Balanced Lunch Box:

Include a variety of food groups such as whole grains, lean proteins, fruits, vegetables, and dairy or dairy alternatives.

Aim for colorful and diverse options to ensure a range of nutrients.

Incorporate foods with different textures and flavors to keep lunches interesting.

Consider portion sizes appropriate for your child's age and activity level.

Pack foods in reusable containers to reduce waste and environmental impact.

Ensure proper food safety by including ice packs for perishable items and storing lunches in insulated lunch boxes.

By prioritizing nutritious choices, adding a dash of creativity, and following these packing tips, you can create lunch boxes that nourish both the body and the imagination of your child. Let's move on to some delicious recipes to bring these ideas to life!

Chapter (1) Sandwiches and Wraps

A. Classic PB&J Roll-Ups:
Ingredients:

- Whole wheat tortillas
- Peanut butter
- Jelly or jam (choose a low-sugar option)

Instructions:

1. Lay a tortilla flat on a clean surface.
2. Spread a layer of peanut butter evenly over the tortilla, leaving a small border around the edges.
3. Spoon jelly or jam over the peanut butter layer.
4. Carefully roll up the tortilla tightly.
5. Use a sharp knife to slice the roll-up into bite-sized pieces.
6. Pack in a lunch box with toothpicks or small skewers for easy eating.

B. Turkey and Cheese Pinwheels:
Ingredients:

- Whole wheat tortillas
- Sliced turkey breast
- Sliced cheese (such as cheddar or Swiss)
- Mustard or mayonnaise (optional)

Instructions:

1. Lay a tortilla flat on a clean surface.
2. Place slices of turkey evenly over the tortilla.
3. Add a layer of cheese on top of the turkey.
4. Optionally, spread a thin layer of mustard or mayonnaise over

the cheese.

5. Roll up the tortilla tightly.
6. Use a sharp knife to slice the roll-up into pinwheels.
7. Secure with toothpicks or small skewers and pack in the lunch box.

C. Veggie Hummus Wraps:
Ingredients:

- Whole wheat wraps or tortillas
- Hummus
- Sliced vegetables (such as cucumbers, carrots, bell peppers, and lettuce)

Instructions:

1. Spread a generous layer of hummus over a whole wheat wrap.
2. Arrange sliced vegetables evenly over the hummus.
3. Roll up the wrap tightly, enclosing the vegetables.
4. Cut the wrap in half or into smaller sections for easier eating.
5. Pack in the lunch box with any additional hummus for dipping.

D. Tuna Salad Sandwiches:
Ingredients:

- Canned tuna, drained
- Mayonnaise
- Diced celery
- Diced onion
- Salt and pepper to taste
- Whole wheat bread slices
- Lettuce leaves (optional)

Instructions:

1. In a bowl, mix together drained tuna, mayonnaise, diced celery, diced onion, salt, and pepper until well combined.
2. Spread the tuna salad mixture onto one slice of whole wheat bread.
3. Optionally, add lettuce leaves on top of the tuna salad.
4. Place another slice of bread on top to form a sandwich.
5. Cut the sandwich in half or into smaller portions if desired.
6. Wrap or pack the sandwiches in the lunch box.

E. Mini Club Sandwich Skewers:
Ingredients:

- Whole wheat bread, toasted
- Sliced turkey breast
- Sliced cheese (such as cheddar or Swiss)
- Lettuce leaves
- Cherry tomatoes
- Toothpicks or small skewers

Instructions:

1. Cut the toasted whole wheat bread into small squares or triangles.
2. Layer a square of bread with a piece of turkey, cheese, lettuce, and cherry tomato.
3. Top with another square of bread to create a mini sandwich.
4. Repeat with remaining ingredients to make additional mini sandwiches.
5. Skewer each mini sandwich with a toothpick or small skewer to hold them together.
6. Arrange the mini club sandwich skewers in the lunch box for easy serving.

Enjoy these tasty and kid-friendly sandwich and wrap options in your child's lunch box!

Chapter (2) Healthy Snacks and Sides

A. Fruit Kabobs with Yogurt Dip:
Ingredients:

- Assorted fruits (such as strawberries, grapes, pineapple chunks, and melon balls)
- Wooden skewers
- Greek yogurt
- Honey (optional)

Instructions:

1. Wash and prepare the fruits by cutting them into bite-sized pieces.
2. Thread the fruit pieces onto wooden skewers, alternating colors and varieties.
3. In a small bowl, mix Greek yogurt with a drizzle of honey if desired for sweetness.
4. Serve the fruit kabobs with the yogurt dip on the side for dipping.

B. Crunchy Veggie Sticks with Ranch Dressing:
Ingredients:

- Assorted raw vegetables (such as carrots, celery, bell peppers, and cucumbers), cut into sticks
- Ranch dressing or dip

Instructions:

1. Wash and cut the vegetables into stick shapes.
2. Arrange the vegetable sticks in a container or bento box.
3. Pour ranch dressing or dip into a small dipping container.

4. Seal the containers and pack them in the lunch box for a crunchy and nutritious snack.

C. Cheese and Crackers Bento Boxes:
Ingredients:

- Assorted cheese slices or cubes (such as cheddar, mozzarella, and Swiss)
- Whole grain crackers
- Sliced fruits (such as apples, grapes, or berries)
- Baby carrots or cucumber slices

Instructions:

1. Arrange cheese slices or cubes and whole grain crackers in a bento box compartment.
2. Add sliced fruits and vegetable sticks in separate compartments.
3. Seal the bento box and pack it in the lunch box for a balanced and satisfying snack.

D. Homemade Granola Bars:
Ingredients:

- 2 cups rolled oats
- 1/2 cup honey or maple syrup
- 1/4 cup peanut butter or almond butter
- 1/4 cup dried fruit (such as raisins, cranberries, or chopped apricots)
- 1/4 cup chopped nuts or seeds (such as almonds, walnuts, or sunflower seeds)
- 1/4 cup chocolate chips (optional)

Instructions:

1. Preheat the oven to 350°F (175°C). Line a baking pan with parchment paper.
2. In a large bowl, mix together oats, honey or maple syrup, peanut butter or almond butter, dried fruit, nuts or seeds, and chocolate chips (if using) until well combined.
3. Press the mixture firmly into the prepared baking pan, spreading it evenly.
4. Bake for 20-25 minutes or until golden brown and firm.
5. Allow the granola bars to cool completely in the pan before cutting them into bars or squares.
6. Wrap the granola bars individually or pack them in an airtight container for a delicious and nutritious snack.

E. Roasted Chickpeas with Seasonings:
Ingredients:

- 1 can (15 ounces) chickpeas, drained and rinsed
- 1 tablespoon olive oil
- Seasonings of choice (such as salt, pepper, garlic powder, paprika, or cumin)

Instructions:

1. Preheat the oven to 400°F (200°C). Line a baking sheet with parchment paper.
2. Pat the chickpeas dry with a paper towel to remove excess moisture.
3. In a bowl, toss the chickpeas with olive oil and seasonings until evenly coated.
4. Spread the seasoned chickpeas in a single layer on the prepared baking sheet.
5. Bake for 25-30 minutes, shaking the pan halfway through, until the chickpeas are crispy and golden brown.

6. Allow the roasted chickpeas to cool before packing them in a container or bento box for a crunchy and protein-packed snack.

These healthy snacks and sides are perfect for keeping your child energized and satisfied throughout the day!

Chapter (3) Creative Bento Boxes

A. Teddy Bear Picnic Bento:
   Ingredients:

- Whole grain bread
- Sliced turkey or ham
- Cheese slices
- Cherry tomatoes
- Baby carrots
- Grapes
- Peanut butter or almond butter
- Honey (optional)
- Edible candy eyes (optional)

Instructions:

1. Use a teddy bear-shaped cookie cutter to cut out sandwiches from whole grain bread.
2. Spread peanut butter or almond butter on one slice of bread and honey on the other slice (optional).
3. Assemble the sandwich with sliced turkey or ham and cheese.
4. Decorate the sandwich with edible candy eyes to create a teddy bear face.
5. Arrange cherry tomatoes, baby carrots, and grapes in the bento box as sides.
6. Pack the teddy bear sandwich and sides in the bento box for a cute and playful lunch.

B. Under the Sea Adventure Bento:
   Ingredients:

- Sushi rice
- Nori (seaweed) sheets
- Cooked shrimp or imitation crab sticks
- Sliced cucumber
- Avocado slices
- Black sesame seeds
- Soy sauce or tamari (for dipping)

Instructions:

1. Shape sushi rice into small balls or rectangles and wrap them with nori strips to resemble seaweed-wrapped sushi.
2. Arrange the sushi rice balls or rectangles in the bento box.
3. Use cooked shrimp or imitation crab sticks to create seafood shapes on top of the rice.
4. Slice cucumber and avocado into thin strips and arrange them around the seafood shapes to resemble seaweed and fish.
5. Sprinkle black sesame seeds over the sushi rice for added texture and decoration.
6. Pack soy sauce or tamari in a small dipping container and include it in the bento box for dipping.

C. Space Explorer Bento:
Ingredients:

- Whole grain pita bread
- Hummus
- Assorted colorful vegetables (such as bell peppers, cherry tomatoes, carrots, and cucumber)
- Sliced cheese (cut into star shapes)
- Sliced fruit (such as strawberries, grapes, and kiwi)
- Yogurt-covered pretzels or dried fruit

Instructions:

1. Cut whole grain pita bread into small triangles to resemble rocket ships.
2. Spread hummus on the pita bread triangles.
3. Arrange colorful vegetables on top of the hummus to create a space-themed design.
4. Use a small cookie cutter to cut sliced cheese into star shapes and place them on toothpicks as "shooting stars."
5. Arrange sliced fruit and yogurt-covered pretzels or dried fruit in the bento box as additional snacks.
6. Pack the space-themed pita sandwiches and snacks in the bento box for a lunch that's out of this world.

D. Rainbow Delight Bento:
Ingredients:

- Cooked quinoa or rice
- Sliced strawberries
- Sliced oranges or mandarin segments
- Sliced pineapple
- Sliced kiwi
- Blueberries
- Purple grapes

Instructions:

1. Divide cooked quinoa or rice into sections in the bento box.
2. Arrange sliced strawberries, oranges or mandarin segments, pineapple, kiwi, blueberries, and grapes in rows over the quinoa or rice, creating a rainbow pattern.
3. Pack a small container of yogurt or honey for dipping fruit if desired.
4. Seal the bento box and pack it for a colorful and nutritious lunch.

E. Farmyard Friends Bento:

Ingredients:

- Whole grain bread
- Sliced deli meat (such as turkey or ham)
- Cheese slices
- Cherry tomatoes
- Sliced cucumbers
- Hard-boiled eggs (peeled and halved)
- Baby carrots
- Black olives

Instructions:

1. Use animal-shaped cookie cutters to cut out sandwiches from whole grain bread.
2. Layer sliced deli meat and cheese between the bread slices to create sandwich animals.
3. Arrange cherry tomatoes, sliced cucumbers, hard-boiled egg halves, baby carrots, and black olives in the bento box to resemble a farmyard scene.
4. Pack the sandwich animals and farmyard-inspired sides in the bento box for a playful and nutritious lunch.

These creative bento box ideas are sure to bring a smile to your child's face and make lunchtime an enjoyable adventure!

Chapter (4) Hot Meals and Leftovers

A. Mini Pizza Muffins:
  Ingredients:

- English muffins, halved
- Pizza sauce
- Shredded mozzarella cheese
- Mini pepperoni slices or diced vegetables (such as bell peppers, mushrooms, and onions)

Instructions:

1. Preheat the oven to 375°F (190°C). Line a muffin tin with paper liners or grease it lightly.
2. Place English muffin halves in the muffin tin.
3. Spread pizza sauce over each English muffin half.
4. Sprinkle shredded mozzarella cheese over the sauce.
5. Add mini pepperoni slices or diced vegetables on top of the cheese.
6. Bake for 10-12 minutes or until the cheese is melted and bubbly.
7. Allow the mini pizza muffins to cool slightly before packing them in a lunch box.

B. Pasta Salad with Veggies:
Ingredients:

- Cooked pasta (such as rotini or penne)
- Cherry tomatoes, halved
- Cucumber, diced
- Bell peppers, diced
- Black olives, sliced
- Feta cheese, crumbled

- Italian dressing

Instructions:

1. In a large bowl, combine cooked pasta, cherry tomatoes, cucumber, bell peppers, black olives, and crumbled feta cheese.
2. Drizzle Italian dressing over the pasta salad and toss gently to coat everything evenly.
3. Pack the pasta salad in a lunch container or bento box with a fork or spoon for easy eating.

C. Chicken Quesadillas:
Ingredients:

- Flour tortillas
- Cooked chicken, shredded or diced
- Shredded cheese (such as cheddar or Monterey Jack)
- Sliced bell peppers
- Sliced onions
- Salsa, sour cream, or guacamole (for dipping)

Instructions:

1. Heat a non-stick skillet over medium heat.
2. Place a flour tortilla in the skillet and sprinkle shredded cheese over one half of the tortilla.
3. Layer cooked chicken, sliced bell peppers, and sliced onions over the cheese.
4. Fold the tortilla in half to cover the filling and press down gently.
5. Cook the quesadilla for 2-3 minutes on each side until the cheese is melted and the tortilla is golden brown.
6. Cut the quesadilla into wedges and serve with salsa, sour cream, or guacamole for dipping.

7. Pack the chicken quesadilla wedges in a lunch box with dipping sauce on the side.

D. Macaroni and Cheese Cups:
Ingredients:

- Elbow macaroni, cooked according to package instructions
- Cheese sauce or homemade cheese sauce
- Bread crumbs (optional)

Instructions:

1. Preheat the oven to 375°F (190°C). Grease a muffin tin or line it with paper liners.
2. In a large bowl, mix cooked elbow macaroni with cheese sauce until well combined.
3. Spoon the macaroni and cheese mixture into the muffin tin, filling each cup about three-quarters full.
4. Optionally, sprinkle bread crumbs on top of each macaroni and cheese cup for added crunch.
5. Bake for 15-20 minutes or until the macaroni and cheese cups are set and golden brown on top.
6. Allow the macaroni and cheese cups to cool slightly before removing them from the muffin tin and packing them in a lunch box.

E. Veggie Fried Rice:
Ingredients:

- Cooked rice (preferably cooled or leftover)
- Mixed vegetables (such as carrots, peas, corn, and bell peppers)
- Diced tofu or cooked chicken (optional)
- Soy sauce or tamari
- Sesame oil

- Scrambled eggs, chopped (optional)

Instructions:

1. Heat a large skillet or wok over medium heat.
2. Add a drizzle of sesame oil to the skillet and stir-fry mixed vegetables until tender-crisp.
3. If using tofu or cooked chicken, add it to the skillet and cook until heated through.
4. Stir in cooked rice and scrambled eggs (if using) and continue to cook, stirring constantly, for 2-3 minutes.
5. Drizzle soy sauce or tamari over the fried rice and toss to coat everything evenly.
6. Allow the fried rice to cool slightly before packing it in a lunch container or bento box.

These hot meals and leftovers are perfect for packing in your child's lunch box and providing them with a satisfying and nutritious meal!

Chapter (5) Sweet Treats and Desserts

A. Banana Sushi Rolls:
Ingredients:

- Bananas
- Peanut butter or almond butter
- Honey (optional)
- Granola
- Mini chocolate chips (optional)

Instructions:

1. Peel a banana and spread a thin layer of peanut butter or almond butter over it.
2. Drizzle honey over the peanut butter (optional).
3. Sprinkle granola and mini chocolate chips (if using) over the peanut butter.
4. Carefully roll the banana in the toppings until coated.
5. Slice the banana into bite-sized sushi rolls.
6. Pack the banana sushi rolls in a lunch box or bento box for a fun and nutritious dessert.

B. Apple Sandwiches with Peanut Butter and Granola:
Ingredients:

- Apples, cored and sliced horizontally into rounds
- Peanut butter or almond butter
- Granola
- Honey (optional)

Instructions:

1. Spread peanut butter or almond butter on one apple slice.

2. Sprinkle granola over the peanut butter.
3. Optionally, drizzle honey over the granola for added sweetness.
4. Top with another apple slice to create a sandwich.
5. Repeat with remaining apple slices.
6. Pack the apple sandwiches in a lunch box for a satisfying and healthy dessert.

C. Yogurt Parfait Cups with Berries:
Ingredients:

- Greek yogurt
- Honey or maple syrup
- Granola
- Fresh berries (such as strawberries, blueberries, and raspberries)

Instructions:

1. In a small cup or container, layer Greek yogurt, honey or maple syrup, granola, and fresh berries.
2. Repeat the layers until the cup is filled.
3. Pack the yogurt parfait cups in a lunch box with a spoon for a delicious and refreshing dessert option.

D. Chocolate Chip Oatmeal Cookies:
Ingredients:

- 1 cup rolled oats
- 1/2 cup whole wheat flour
- 1/4 cup coconut oil, melted
- 1/4 cup maple syrup or honey
- 1/4 cup mini chocolate chips
- 1 egg (or flax egg for vegan option)

- 1/2 teaspoon vanilla extract
- 1/4 teaspoon baking soda
- Pinch of salt

Instructions:

1. Preheat the oven to 350°F (175°C). Line a baking sheet with parchment paper.
2. In a large bowl, mix together rolled oats, whole wheat flour, melted coconut oil, maple syrup or honey, mini chocolate chips, egg, vanilla extract, baking soda, and salt until well combined.
3. Drop spoonfuls of cookie dough onto the prepared baking sheet, spacing them apart.
4. Flatten each cookie slightly with the back of a spoon.
5. Bake for 10-12 minutes or until the cookies are golden brown around the edges.
6. Allow the cookies to cool on the baking sheet for a few minutes before transferring them to a wire rack to cool completely.
7. Once cooled, pack the chocolate chip oatmeal cookies in a lunch box for a sweet treat.

E. Mini Muffins with Hidden Veggies:
   Ingredients:

- 1 cup all-purpose flour
- 1/2 cup whole wheat flour
- 1/4 cup sugar
- 1 teaspoon baking powder
- 1/2 teaspoon baking soda
- 1/4 teaspoon salt
- 1/2 cup unsweetened applesauce
- 1/4 cup milk (or plant-based milk)

- 2 tablespoons coconut oil, melted
- 1 teaspoon vanilla extract
- 1 cup finely grated zucchini or carrots
- Optional add-ins: shredded coconut, chopped nuts, or mini chocolate chips

Instructions:

1. Preheat the oven to 350°F (175°C). Grease a mini muffin tin or line it with paper liners.
2. In a large bowl, whisk together all-purpose flour, whole wheat flour, sugar, baking powder, baking soda, and salt.
3. In a separate bowl, mix together applesauce, milk, melted coconut oil, and vanilla extract until well combined.
4. Pour the wet ingredients into the dry ingredients and stir until just combined.
5. Fold in finely grated zucchini or carrots and any optional add-ins until evenly distributed.
6. Spoon the batter into the prepared mini muffin tin, filling each cavity about three-quarters full.
7. Bake for 12-15 minutes or until a toothpick inserted into the center of a muffin comes out clean.
8. Allow the mini muffins to cool in the tin for a few minutes before transferring them to a wire rack to cool completely.
9. Once cooled, pack the mini muffins in a lunch box for a nutritious and sneaky way to eat veggies.

These sweet treats and desserts are perfect for satisfying your child's sweet tooth while providing them with wholesome ingredients. Enjoy!

Chapter (6) Allergy-Friendly Options

A. Gluten-Free Sandwich Ideas:
Ingredients:

- Gluten-free bread slices or wraps

Fillings such as:

- Sliced deli meat (ensure it's gluten-free)
- Dairy-free cheese
- Lettuce, tomato, and other vegetables
- Hummus or avocado spread

Instructions:

1. Use gluten-free bread slices or wraps as the base for sandwiches.
2. Fill the sandwiches with your choice of gluten-free fillings, such as sliced deli meat, dairy-free cheese, fresh vegetables, and spreads like hummus or avocado.
3. Customize the sandwiches to your child's preferences and pack them safely in a lunch box.

B. Nut-Free Snacks and Treats:
Options:

- Fresh fruit slices or fruit cups
- Veggie sticks with hummus or ranch dressing
- Popcorn
- Rice cakes or rice crackers with toppings like sunflower seed butter or dairy-free cream cheese
- Pretzels
- Gluten-free granola bars (ensure they're nut-free)

- Dairy-free yogurt or yogurt tubes

Instructions:

1. Choose snacks and treats that are labeled nut-free or made in nut-free facilities to ensure safety for children with nut allergies.
2. Pack these options in a lunch box or bento box, ensuring they are stored separately from any nut-containing foods to prevent cross-contamination.

C. Dairy-Free Lunch Box Alternatives:
Options:

- Dairy-free sandwiches or wraps made with alternatives like hummus, avocado, or dairy-free cheese
- Veggie sticks with dairy-free ranch dressing or hummus
- Fresh fruit slices or fruit cups
- Dairy-free yogurt or yogurt tubes
- Rice cakes or rice crackers with toppings like sunflower seed butter or dairy-free cream cheese
- Gluten-free granola bars (ensure they're dairy-free)

Instructions:

1. Opt for dairy-free alternatives in sandwiches, snacks, and treats to accommodate children with dairy allergies or lactose intolerance.
2. Ensure that any dairy substitutes are clearly labeled dairy-free and free from cross-contamination with dairy products.

D. Egg-Free Options for Meals:
Options:

- Vegetable stir-fry with tofu or tempeh

- Bean or lentil-based salads with mixed vegetables and a vinaigrette dressing
- Pasta with marinara sauce and roasted vegetables
- Rice or quinoa bowls with black beans, corn, avocado, and salsa
- Veggie burgers or falafel wraps with dairy-free tzatziki sauce

Instructions:

1. Prepare meals using plant-based proteins and avoid using eggs or egg-containing ingredients to accommodate children with egg allergies.
2. Check food labels carefully to ensure that packaged foods do not contain eggs or traces of eggs.

E. Vegan Lunch Box Inspirations:
Options:

- Vegan sandwiches or wraps filled with hummus, falafel, grilled vegetables, or avocado
- Quinoa or rice salads with mixed vegetables, beans, and a citrus vinaigrette
- Vegan sushi rolls made with vegetables, tofu, or avocado
- Lentil or chickpea salads with herbs, tomatoes, and a lemon tahini dressing
- Vegan protein balls or energy bites made with oats, nut butter alternatives, seeds, and dried fruit

Instructions:

1. Create plant-based meals and snacks that are free from animal products to accommodate vegan dietary preferences.
2. Incorporate a variety of flavors, textures, and colors to make vegan lunch boxes vibrant and satisfying.

These allergy-friendly options provide safe and delicious choices for children with dietary restrictions or allergies, ensuring that everyone can enjoy a tasty and nutritious lunch.

Chapter (7) Quick and Easy Prep Tips

A. Sunday Meal Prep Ideas:
Suggestions:

- Prepare a large batch of grains like quinoa, rice, or couscous to use as a base for various meals throughout the week.
- Cook a protein source such as grilled chicken, tofu, or beans to incorporate into salads, sandwiches, or wraps.
- Wash and chop a variety of vegetables to have them ready for quick snacks, salads, stir-fries, or side dishes.
- Make a big pot of soup, stew, or chili that can be portioned out and frozen for easy reheating during the week.
- Bake a batch of muffins, energy bars, or cookies for grab-and-go snacks or desserts.

B. Time-Saving Strategies for Busy Parents:
Tips:

- Plan meals for the week ahead of time to streamline grocery shopping and meal prep.
- Use kitchen gadgets like slow cookers, pressure cookers, or air fryers to cut down on cooking time.
- Prep ingredients in batches when you have some free time, such as washing and cutting vegetables or marinating proteins.
- Keep a well-stocked pantry with staple ingredients like canned beans, diced tomatoes, pasta, and grains for quick and easy meal assembly.
- Double recipes and freeze leftovers for future meals to save time on busy days.

C. Batch Cooking for Convenient Lunch Box Packing:
Ideas:

- Cook large batches of soups, stews, or casseroles that can be portioned out into individual containers for easy grab-and-go lunches.
- Make a big batch of roasted vegetables, grains, or protein sources like chicken or tofu to mix and match throughout the week.
- Prep components of meals ahead of time, such as chopping vegetables or cooking rice, to speed up assembly during the week.
- Use silicone muffin cups to portion out snacks like trail mix, granola, or chopped fruits for easy packing into lunch boxes.

D. Freezing and Thawing Guidelines:
Freezing Tips:

- Cool cooked foods completely before freezing to prevent ice crystals from forming.
- Store foods in airtight containers or freezer bags to prevent freezer burn.
- Label containers with the date and contents for easy identification.

Thawing Tips:

- Thaw frozen meals in the refrigerator overnight for safe and even thawing.
- Use the defrost setting on the microwave for quicker thawing of individual portions.
- For soups or stews, thaw in a pot on the stove over low heat, stirring occasionally until fully thawed and heated through.

E. Packing Tips to Keep Food Fresh:

Suggestions:

- Use insulated lunch boxes or bags to keep food at the proper temperature until lunchtime.
- Pack perishable items like sandwiches or yogurt cups with ice packs to keep them cold.
- Use leak-proof containers for liquids like soups or dressings to prevent spills.
- Pack crunchy items like chips or crackers separately from moist foods to maintain their texture.
- Encourage your child to eat perishable items like dairy products or meats first to ensure food safety.

By implementing these quick and easy prep tips, you can save time and effort while ensuring that your child's lunches are nutritious, delicious, and convenient for busy weekdays.

Chapter (8) International Flavors

A. Japanese Bento Box with Onigiri and Teriyaki Chicken:

- Onigiri: Cook sushi rice according to package instructions. Shape the rice into triangles or balls, and place a filling such as pickled plum, grilled salmon, or tuna mayo in the center. Wrap each onigiri with a strip of nori seaweed.
- Teriyaki Chicken: Marinate chicken breast strips in a mixture of soy sauce, mirin, sake (optional), grated ginger, and garlic for at least 30 minutes. Cook the marinated chicken in a skillet until cooked through, then brush with teriyaki sauce.
- Pack the onigiri and teriyaki chicken in a bento box along with steamed broccoli or edamame for a complete Japanese-inspired meal.

B. Mexican Fiesta: Taco Salad Cups and Mini Quesadilla Triangles:

- Taco Salad Cups: Line muffin cups with tortilla wraps and bake until crispy to form edible cups. Fill each cup with a mixture of seasoned ground beef or turkey, black beans, corn, diced tomatoes, shredded lettuce, diced avocado, and shredded cheese. Top with salsa and a dollop of sour cream.
- Mini Quesadilla Triangles: Spread refried beans and shredded cheese onto small flour tortillas. Top with another tortilla and press down gently. Cook the quesadillas in a skillet until the cheese is melted and the tortillas are crispy. Cut into triangles.
- Pack the taco salad cups and mini quesadilla triangles in a lunch box along with guacamole, salsa, and tortilla chips for a festive Mexican-inspired meal.

C. Italian Delights: Caprese Skewers and Mini Meatball Subs:

- Caprese Skewers: Thread cherry tomatoes, fresh mozzarella balls, and basil leaves onto skewers. Drizzle with balsamic glaze and sprinkle with salt and pepper.
- Mini Meatball Subs: Prepare mini meatballs using a mixture of ground beef or turkey, breadcrumbs, Parmesan cheese, egg, minced garlic, Italian seasoning, salt, and pepper. Bake the meatballs until cooked through, then place them in mini sub rolls with marinara sauce and shredded mozzarella cheese.
- Pack the caprese skewers and mini meatball subs in a lunch box along with a side of mixed greens dressed with olive oil and balsamic vinegar for an Italian-inspired meal.

D. Mediterranean Mezze Platter: Hummus, Falafel, and Pita Bread:

- Hummus: Serve store-bought or homemade hummus with a drizzle of olive oil and a sprinkle of paprika. Include cucumber and carrot sticks for dipping.
- Falafel: Form chickpea mixture into small balls and deep-fry or bake until golden brown and crispy. Serve with tahini sauce or tzatziki.
- Pita Bread: Warm pita bread in the oven or toaster and cut into triangles for dipping.
- Pack the hummus, falafel, and pita bread in a lunch box along with sliced tomatoes, olives, and feta cheese for a Mediterranean-inspired mezze platter.

E. Indian Spice Adventure: Veggie Samosas and Mango Lassi Popsicles:

- Veggie Samosas: Fill store-bought or homemade pastry dough with a mixture of potatoes, peas, carrots, onions, and spices such as cumin, coriander, turmeric, and garam masala. Bake or fry until golden brown and crispy.

- Mango Lassi Popsicles: Blend mango chunks, yogurt, milk, honey, and a pinch of cardamom until smooth. Pour the mixture into popsicle molds and freeze until solid.
- Pack the veggie samosas and mango lassi popsicles in a lunch box along with basmati rice and a side of mint chutney for an adventurous Indian-inspired meal.

These international flavors provide a delicious and diverse array of options to add excitement and variety to your child's lunchtime experience. Enjoy exploring different cuisines from around the world!

Chapter (9) Seasonal Specials

A. Springtime Salad Jars with Fresh Greens and Strawberries:
Ingredients:

- Mixed salad greens (such as spinach, arugula, and lettuce)
- Sliced strawberries
- Sliced almonds
- Feta cheese
- Balsamic vinaigrette

Instructions:

1. Layer mixed salad greens, sliced strawberries, sliced almonds, and crumbled feta cheese in Mason jars.
2. Seal the jars and pack them in a lunch box with a small container of balsamic vinaigrette for a fresh and portable springtime salad.

B. Summer Picnic Favorites: Watermelon Pizza and Cucumber Sandwiches:
Watermelon Pizza:

- Slice watermelon into rounds to resemble pizza crust.
- Top with Greek yogurt or dairy-free yogurt, sliced fruits (such as berries, kiwi, and mango), and a sprinkle of granola or shredded coconut.

Cucumber Sandwiches:

- Spread cream cheese or dairy-free cream cheese on cucumber slices.

- Top with thinly sliced turkey or smoked salmon and another cucumber slice to form sandwiches.
- Pack the watermelon pizza slices and cucumber sandwiches in a lunch box along with carrot sticks and hummus for a refreshing summer picnic spread.

C. Autumn Harvest: Butternut Squash Soup Shots and Pumpkin Muffins:

Butternut Squash Soup Shots:

- Prepare butternut squash soup with flavors of cinnamon, nutmeg, and a touch of cream or coconut milk.
- Pour the soup into small shot glasses or thermos flasks for easy sipping.

Pumpkin Muffins:

- Bake pumpkin muffins with pumpkin puree, spices (such as cinnamon, nutmeg, and cloves), and chocolate chips or chopped nuts.
- Pack the butternut squash soup shots and pumpkin muffins in a lunch box along with apple slices and cinnamon for a cozy autumn-inspired meal.

D. Winter Warmers: Chicken Noodle Soup in Thermos Flasks and Hot Cocoa Mix:

Chicken Noodle Soup:

- Prepare homemade chicken noodle soup with tender chicken, vegetables, and noodles in a flavorful broth.
- Ladle the soup into thermos flasks to keep it warm until lunchtime.

Hot Cocoa Mix:

- Mix together cocoa powder, sugar, and powdered milk or dairy-free milk powder.
- Pack the hot cocoa mix in small containers along with mini marshmallows or whipped cream for a comforting winter treat.
- Pack the thermos flasks of chicken noodle soup and containers of hot cocoa mix in a lunch box along with crackers or breadsticks for dipping.

E. Holiday-themed Treats: Christmas Tree Sandwiches and Halloween Ghost Cookies:
Christmas Tree Sandwiches:

- Use a Christmas tree-shaped cookie cutter to cut sandwiches from bread slices.
- Fill the sandwiches with holiday-themed ingredients like turkey, cranberry sauce, and cheese.

Halloween Ghost Cookies:

- Bake sugar cookies in ghost shapes and decorate with white icing or melted white chocolate to create spooky faces.
- Pack the Christmas tree sandwiches and Halloween ghost cookies in a lunch box along with festive fruit skewers (such as grapes and kiwi) and a small container of yogurt dip for dipping.

These seasonal specials are sure to delight your child's taste buds and bring a touch of the season to their lunchtime experience. Enjoy the flavors and festivities of each season!

Chapter (10) Edible Art and Food Crafts

A. Sandwich Sculptures: Animal Faces and Fun Shapes:

- Use cookie cutters to create fun shapes like stars, hearts, or dinosaurs from bread slices.
- Decorate sandwiches with ingredients like sliced cheese, deli meats, and vegetables to form animal faces or playful scenes.
- Add details using food-safe markers or small pieces of fruits and vegetables for eyes, noses, and mouths.

B. Food Painting: Edible Ink and Veggie Brushes:

- Create edible paint by mixing food coloring with a small amount of water or milk.
- Use clean paintbrushes to paint designs on bread, cookies, or tortillas.
- Experiment with natural food dyes made from ingredients like beets, spinach, or turmeric for vibrant colors.

C. Rice Krispies Treats Creations: 3D Characters and Scenes:

- Mold Rice Krispies treats into shapes like animals, flowers, or buildings using your hands or cookie cutters.
- Use icing or melted chocolate to add details and decorate the treats.
- Arrange the treats to create 3D scenes or dioramas, such as a jungle with animals or a city skyline.

D. Cookie Decorating: Frosting and Sprinkle Designs:

- Bake sugar cookies in various shapes like hearts, stars, or animals.

- Use frosting in different colors to pipe designs onto the cookies, such as swirls, dots, or stripes.
- Sprinkle edible decorations like colored sugar, sprinkles, or edible glitter to add texture and sparkle.

E. Fruit Carving: Watermelon Whales and Apple Swans:

- Carve watermelon into whale shapes by cutting away sections to create fins and a tail.
- Use a melon baller to scoop out the flesh and create the whale's eye.
- Carve apples into swan shapes by cutting a notch for the head and using a small knife to shape the neck and body.
- Use toothpicks to attach small pieces of fruit, such as grapes or berries, for the swan's features and feathers.

These edible art and food craft ideas are not only fun to make but also add a creative and playful element to mealtime. Let your child's imagination run wild as they explore different techniques and create their own edible masterpieces!

Chapter (11) Interactive Lunches

A. Build-Your-Own Sandwich Bar with Assorted Fillings and Toppings:

- Set up a variety of bread options, such as sliced bread, rolls, and wraps.
- Provide an assortment of fillings such as deli meats, cheese slices, hummus, tuna salad, and grilled vegetables.
- Offer toppings like lettuce, tomatoes, cucumbers, onions, pickles, olives, and condiments.
- Let each child customize their sandwich with their favorite ingredients.

B. DIY Pizza Pockets: Individual Dough and Topping Stations:

- Prepare individual portions of pizza dough or use pre-made dough.
- Set up stations with a variety of toppings such as pizza sauce, cheese, pepperoni, diced vegetables, and cooked sausage or chicken.
- Let each child roll out their portion of dough and add their desired toppings.
- Fold the dough over the toppings to create pockets and seal the edges.
- Bake the pizza pockets until golden brown and bubbly.

C. Salad Bowl Assembly: Mix and Match Ingredients for Customized Salads:

- Offer a selection of salad greens such as spinach, lettuce, arugula, and mixed greens.

- Provide a variety of toppings such as chopped vegetables, beans, nuts, seeds, cheese, croutons, and grilled chicken or tofu.
- Offer a selection of dressings such as vinaigrettes, ranch, Caesar, or balsamic glaze.
- Let each child build their own salad by choosing their favorite ingredients and dressings.

D. Taco Tuesday: Tortilla Wraps, Fillings, and Salsa Bar:

- Set up a taco bar with tortillas, both hard and soft, as well as lettuce wraps for a low-carb option.
- Provide a variety of fillings such as seasoned ground beef or turkey, shredded chicken, black beans, sautéed vegetables, and rice.
- Offer toppings like shredded cheese, diced tomatoes, sliced onions, shredded lettuce, guacamole, sour cream, and salsa.
- Let each child assemble their own tacos or wraps with their preferred fillings and toppings.

E. Sushi Rolling Party: Nori, Rice, and Various Fillings for Homemade Sushi Rolls:

- Provide sushi rolling mats, nori sheets, sushi rice, and a selection of fillings such as cucumber, avocado, crab sticks, cooked shrimp, smoked salmon, and tofu.
- Offer condiments like soy sauce, wasabi, and pickled ginger.
- Let each child assemble their own sushi rolls by spreading rice on the nori, adding their chosen fillings, and rolling it up using the sushi mat.
- Encourage creativity with different combinations of fillings and rolling techniques.

These interactive lunch ideas are not only fun and engaging but also allow children to explore different flavors and textures while developing their culinary skills. Enjoy the interactive lunchtime experience!

Chapter (12) Cooking with Kids

A. Child-Friendly Recipes for Little Helpers:

- Choose simple recipes with few ingredients and easy-to-follow instructions.
- Opt for recipes that involve kid-friendly tasks such as mixing, stirring, rolling, and shaping.
- Examples include fruit skewers, homemade granola bars, mini pizzas, pasta salads, and smoothie bowls.

B. Kitchen Safety Tips and Guidelines:

- Teach children basic kitchen safety rules such as washing hands before cooking, using oven mitts when handling hot items, and staying away from sharp objects.
- Supervise children closely while they're in the kitchen, especially when using appliances or cooking on the stove.
- Show children how to properly use kitchen tools and equipment to prevent accidents.

C. Fun Cooking Activities to Engage Children:

- Turn cooking into a fun and educational experience by involving children in every step of the process.
- Encourage creativity by letting children choose ingredients, experiment with flavors, and decorate their creations.
- Some fun cooking activities include baking cookies, making homemade pizza, assembling taco bars, decorating cupcakes, and creating fruit salads.

D. Teaching Healthy Eating Habits Through Cooking:

- Use cooking as an opportunity to teach children about the

importance of nutritious eating habits.

- Discuss the benefits of incorporating fruits, vegetables, whole grains, and lean proteins into their diet.
- Encourage children to try new foods and explore different flavors while cooking together.

E. Building Confidence and Creativity in the Kitchen:

- Allow children to take on age-appropriate tasks and responsibilities in the kitchen to build their confidence and independence.
- Praise children for their efforts and celebrate their accomplishments, no matter how small.
- Encourage creativity by letting children express themselves through cooking and experiment with new ingredients and techniques.

By cooking with kids and involving them in the kitchen, you can not only create delicious meals together but also teach valuable life skills, promote healthy eating habits, and foster creativity and confidence in your little chefs. Enjoy the bonding experience and culinary adventures with your children!

Chapter (13) Leftover Makeovers

A. Reinventing Dinner Leftovers into Lunchbox Masterpieces:

- Use leftover proteins like grilled chicken, steak, or tofu to create sandwiches, wraps, or salads for lunchboxes.
- Turn leftover vegetables into frittatas, quiches, or veggie-packed muffins.
- Transform leftover grains like rice or quinoa into grain bowls or fried rice with added vegetables and protein.

B. Transforming Roast Chicken into Chicken Salad Wraps:

- Shred leftover roast chicken and mix it with mayonnaise or Greek yogurt, diced celery, grapes, and nuts to make chicken salad.
- Spread the chicken salad onto tortillas or wraps, add lettuce or spinach leaves, and roll them up for easy chicken salad wraps.

C. Remixing Pasta Dishes into Pasta Salads:

- Turn leftover pasta dishes like spaghetti or penne into pasta salads by adding fresh vegetables, cheese, and a vinaigrette dressing.
- Mix in ingredients like cherry tomatoes, cucumbers, bell peppers, olives, and herbs for added flavor and texture.

D. Making Soup from Scratch Using Remaining Ingredients:

- Use leftover meats, vegetables, and grains to make a hearty soup or stew.
- Simmer the ingredients with broth or stock, seasonings, and herbs until flavors meld together to create a comforting and nutritious meal.

E. Creative Ways to Utilize Extra Fruits and Vegetables:

- Make smoothies using leftover fruits, yogurt, and milk or juice.
- Bake fruits into muffins, bread, or oatmeal for a delicious breakfast or snack.
- Roast vegetables and toss them with grains or salads for added flavor and nutrition.
- Blend leftover vegetables into soups, sauces, or dips for extra vitamins and minerals.

These leftover makeover ideas help reduce food waste while creating delicious and nutritious meals for lunch or dinner. Get creative with your leftovers and enjoy the tasty results!

Chapter (14) All-Time Favorites Reinvented

A. Healthier Versions of Classic Lunchbox Treats:

- Replace traditional ingredients with healthier alternatives, such as using whole wheat flour instead of white flour in muffins or cookies.
- Reduce added sugars by sweetening treats with natural sweeteners like honey, maple syrup, or mashed bananas.
- Incorporate nutrient-rich ingredients like oats, nuts, seeds, and dried fruits for added texture and flavor.

B. Low-Sugar Options for Traditional Desserts:

- Use unsweetened applesauce or mashed ripe bananas to replace some or all of the sugar in recipes like cakes, brownies, or cookies.
- Opt for natural sweeteners like stevia, monk fruit sweetener, or erythritol in place of refined sugars.
- Experiment with flavorings like vanilla extract, cinnamon, or citrus zest to enhance sweetness without adding extra sugar.

C. Sneaky Veggie Additions to Familiar Dishes:

- Grate vegetables like carrots, zucchini, or spinach into dishes such as muffins, pancakes, or pasta sauces for added moisture and nutrients.
- Blend vegetables into smoothies or soups to boost their nutritional content without altering the taste.
- Incorporate pureed vegetables like cauliflower or sweet potatoes into creamy sauces or dips for a hidden veggie boost.

D. Whole Grain Alternatives to Standard Ingredients:

- Substitute whole wheat flour or oat flour for white flour in recipes like pancakes, waffles, or bread.
- Use whole grain pasta or brown rice instead of refined grains in dishes like pasta salads, stir-fries, or casseroles.
- Choose whole grain cereals or granola bars for snacks instead of sugary, refined options.

E. Balancing Nostalgia with Nutritional Value:

- Maintain the familiar flavors and textures of favorite dishes while incorporating healthier ingredients.
- Emphasize portion control and moderation to enjoy nostalgic treats without compromising nutritional goals.
- Encourage mindful eating practices by savoring nostalgic foods and appreciating the memories associated with them.

By reinventing all-time favorites with healthier ingredients and mindful preparation techniques, you can enjoy the comfort and nostalgia of beloved dishes while promoting better nutrition and overall well-being.

Chapter (15) On-the-Go Options

A. Portable Lunch Ideas for Busy Days:

- Prepare grab-and-go options like wraps, sandwiches, or salads in advance for quick and convenient lunches.
- Pack snack boxes with a variety of healthy options such as cut-up fruits and vegetables, cheese cubes, crackers, and nuts.
- Make homemade energy bars or muffins for a portable and satisfying snack on busy days.

B. Easy-to-Pack Meals for Field Trips and Outings:

- Opt for foods that are easy to eat with minimal mess, such as sandwiches, wraps, or sushi rolls.
- Pack pre-portioned snacks like trail mix, fruit slices, or yogurt cups in individual containers for easy snacking on the go.
- Bring reusable water bottles to stay hydrated throughout the day.

C. Tips for Keeping Food Fresh without Refrigeration:

- Use insulated lunch bags or coolers with ice packs to keep perishable items like sandwiches, salads, and yogurt cold.
- Pack foods in airtight containers to prevent them from spoiling or leaking.
- Choose shelf-stable options like whole fruits, nuts, granola bars, and dried fruit for snacks that don't require refrigeration.

D. Convenient Containers and Lunchbox Accessories:

- Invest in durable and leak-proof containers that are suitable for packing a variety of foods.

- Consider bento boxes or compartmentalized containers to keep different foods separate and organized.
- Pack reusable utensils, napkins, and water bottles to minimize waste and make eating on the go more convenient.

E. Making Healthy Choices While Traveling:

- Plan ahead and pack nutritious snacks like fresh fruit, vegetables, nuts, and whole grain crackers to avoid relying on unhealthy options while traveling.
- Choose restaurants or cafes that offer healthy menu choices such as salads, grilled proteins, and vegetable-based dishes.
- Stay hydrated by drinking plenty of water and limiting sugary beverages like soda or juice while traveling.

By incorporating these on-the-go options and strategies into your routine, you can enjoy healthy and satisfying meals and snacks no matter how busy your schedule or where your travels take you.

Chapter (16) Cooking for Picky Eaters

A. Strategies for Introducing New Foods to Selective Palates:

- Start small by introducing new foods alongside familiar favorites.
- Offer foods in different forms (raw, cooked, blended) to see what your child prefers.
- Make mealtimes relaxed and positive, without pressure or coercion to try new foods.

B. Hiding Nutrients in Kid-Friendly Recipes:

- Sneak vegetables into dishes by pureeing them and adding them to sauces, soups, or baked goods.
- Incorporate fruits and vegetables into smoothies or homemade popsicles.
- Use whole grain flours and oats in baking to boost fiber content.

C. Engaging Children in the Meal Planning Process:

- Involve children in grocery shopping and let them choose fruits, vegetables, and other ingredients.
- Allow children to help with meal preparation, such as washing vegetables, stirring ingredients, or assembling dishes.
- Encourage children to suggest meal ideas and be open to trying new recipes together.

D. Dealing with Texture and Temperature Preferences:

- Offer a variety of textures in meals, such as crunchy, smooth, and chewy.
- Respect your child's temperature preferences by serving warm and cold foods based on their preferences.

- Be patient and continue to expose your child to different textures over time.

E. Celebrating Small Victories in Expanding Taste Preferences:

- Praise and encourage your child when they try new foods, even if they don't like them at first.
- Acknowledge and celebrate small victories, such as trying a new fruit or vegetable or eating a food in a different form.
- Keep a positive attitude and focus on progress rather than perfection.

By implementing these strategies and approaches, you can help picky eaters develop a more varied and nutritious diet while fostering a positive relationship with food. Remember to be patient, consistent, and supportive throughout the process of expanding your child's taste preferences.

Chapter (17) All About Dips and Sauces

A. DIY Recipes for Homemade Condiments:

- Prepare homemade ketchup using tomato paste, vinegar, sweetener (such as honey or maple syrup), and spices like garlic powder, onion powder, and paprika.
- Make your own barbecue sauce by combining tomato sauce, apple cider vinegar, molasses, Worcestershire sauce, and spices like chili powder, cumin, and mustard powder.
- Create a creamy ranch dressing with Greek yogurt, mayonnaise, fresh herbs (such as dill and parsley), garlic powder, onion powder, and lemon juice.

B. Versatile Dips for Veggies, Chips, and Sandwiches:

- Whip up a classic hummus using canned chickpeas, tahini, lemon juice, garlic, and olive oil, perfect for dipping vegetables, pita bread, or crackers.
- Prepare a creamy avocado dip by mashing ripe avocados with lime juice, salt, pepper, and optional add-ins like diced tomatoes, red onion, and cilantro.
- Mix together a tangy tzatziki sauce with Greek yogurt, grated cucumber, garlic, lemon juice, and fresh dill, ideal for serving with grilled meats, falafel, or as a dip for pita chips.

C. Healthy Alternatives to Store-Bought Sauces:

- Replace store-bought pasta sauce with homemade marinara made from canned tomatoes, garlic, onions, olive oil, and Italian herbs, reducing added sugars and preservatives.
- Swap out store-bought teriyaki sauce for a homemade version using soy sauce, honey or maple syrup, garlic, ginger, and sesame

oil, controlling the amount of sodium and sweeteners.

- Opt for homemade salsa made with fresh tomatoes, onions, jalapeños, cilantro, lime juice, and salt, avoiding additives and preservatives found in commercial varieties.

D. Tips for Making Creamy Dressings without Dairy:

- Use plant-based alternatives like cashews or silken tofu blended with water, lemon juice, vinegar, and herbs to create creamy dressings without dairy.
- Make a creamy tahini dressing by combining tahini paste with water, lemon juice, garlic, salt, and pepper for a dairy-free option with a nutty flavor.
- Experiment with avocado-based dressings by blending ripe avocados with olive oil, vinegar or citrus juice, and seasonings to achieve a smooth and creamy texture without dairy.

E. Enhancing Flavor Profiles with Simple Sauces:

- Elevate grilled meats or vegetables with a chimichurri sauce made from fresh herbs (such as parsley, cilantro, and oregano), garlic, red wine vinegar, olive oil, and red pepper flakes.
- Add depth to stir-fries or rice bowls with a homemade teriyaki glaze consisting of soy sauce, brown sugar, ginger, garlic, and cornstarch for thickening.
- Drizzle roasted vegetables or salads with a balsamic glaze made from balsamic vinegar and honey, reducing it on the stove until thick and syrupy for a sweet and tangy finish.

These homemade dips and sauces offer delicious alternatives to store-bought varieties, allowing you to control the ingredients and customize flavors to suit your taste preferences and dietary needs. Experiment with different recipes and enjoy the versatility and flavor-enhancing qualities they bring to your meals.

Chapter (18) Special Dietary Needs and Restrictions

A. Catering to Gluten-Free Diets with Flavorful Alternatives:

- Replace wheat flour with gluten-free alternatives such as almond flour, coconut flour, or a gluten-free flour blend in recipes for baked goods like muffins, pancakes, and cookies.
- Use naturally gluten-free grains like quinoa, rice, and oats as substitutes for pasta, couscous, and bulgur in savory dishes and salads.
- Experiment with gluten-free grains like amaranth, millet, and sorghum to add variety and texture to meals.

B. Nutrient-Rich Recipes for Vegetarian and Vegan Kids:

- Incorporate plant-based protein sources like beans, lentils, tofu, tempeh, and edamame into meals such as stir-fries, curries, and salads.
- Include plenty of fruits, vegetables, whole grains, nuts, and seeds to ensure a balanced and nutritious diet for vegetarian and vegan children.
- Explore vegetarian and vegan versions of classic dishes such as vegetable lasagna, black bean burgers, and chickpea curry.

C. Managing Food Allergies with Safe Substitutions:

- Replace allergenic ingredients like dairy, eggs, nuts, and soy with suitable alternatives such as dairy-free milk, egg replacers, seed butters, and coconut aminos in recipes.
- Check food labels carefully and be vigilant about cross-contamination when cooking for children with food allergies to ensure their safety.

- Communicate openly with caregivers, teachers, and other parents about your child's food allergies to prevent accidental exposure to allergens.

D. Low-Carb Lunchbox Ideas for Keto-Friendly Eating:

- Pack protein-rich snacks like hard-boiled eggs, cheese cubes, deli meat roll-ups, and Greek yogurt with nuts for keto-friendly options that keep kids satisfied throughout the day.
- Include low-carb vegetables like bell pepper strips, cucumber slices, cherry tomatoes, and celery sticks with hummus or guacamole for crunchy and nutritious snacks.
- Prepare keto-friendly wraps or lettuce wraps filled with sliced turkey, cheese, avocado, and leafy greens for a portable and satisfying lunch option.

E. Adapting Recipes for Specific Dietary Preferences and Requirements:

- Modify recipes to accommodate specific dietary preferences and requirements by substituting ingredients or adjusting cooking methods.
- Offer a variety of options and alternatives to cater to individual tastes and preferences within the family, whether it's gluten-free, dairy-free, vegetarian, or low-carb.
- Be flexible and creative in the kitchen, experimenting with different ingredients and techniques to create delicious and satisfying meals for everyone.

By being mindful of special dietary needs and restrictions, you can ensure that all children have access to nutritious and enjoyable meals that meet their individual requirements and preferences. With a bit of planning and creativity, you can accommodate a variety of dietary needs while still providing delicious and satisfying meals for kids.

Chapter (19) Sustainable Lunches

A. Tips for Reducing Packaging Waste in Lunchboxes:

- Use reusable containers and utensils instead of single-use plastic bags and disposable cutlery.
- Pack lunches in bento boxes or compartmentalized containers to minimize the need for additional packaging.
- Choose snacks that come in bulk or larger packages and portion them into reusable containers to reduce individual packaging waste.

B. Eco-Friendly Alternatives to Single-Use Plastics:

- Invest in reusable sandwich wraps, snack bags, and drink bottles made from materials like silicone, stainless steel, or glass.
- Avoid single-use plastic bags, cling wrap, and disposable water bottles by opting for eco-friendly alternatives that can be reused multiple times.
- Look for biodegradable or compostable options for disposable items when reusable alternatives are not feasible.

C. Incorporating Locally Sourced and Seasonal Ingredients:

- Shop for ingredients at local farmers' markets or farms to reduce carbon emissions associated with transportation and support the local economy.
- Choose seasonal fruits and vegetables that are grown locally and require fewer resources for cultivation and preservation.
- Consider joining a community-supported agriculture (CSA) program to receive fresh, seasonal produce directly from local farmers on a regular basis.

D. Plant-Based Meal Ideas for Lower Environmental Impact:

- Incorporate more plant-based meals into lunchboxes by including options like veggie wraps, quinoa salads, bean burritos, or lentil soup.
- Experiment with plant-based proteins such as tofu, tempeh, beans, lentils, and chickpeas as alternatives to meat and dairy products.
- Reduce the carbon footprint of meals by choosing plant-based ingredients that require fewer resources to produce compared to animal products.

E. Teaching Children about the Importance of Sustainability through Food Choices:

- Engage children in discussions about where their food comes from, how it's produced, and the environmental impact of different food choices.
- Involve children in meal planning, shopping, and cooking activities to help them develop a deeper understanding of sustainable food practices.
- Encourage children to make eco-friendly choices by explaining the benefits of reducing waste, supporting local farmers, and choosing plant-based foods.

By incorporating sustainable practices into lunchtime routines and teaching children about the importance of environmental stewardship through food choices, you can help promote a healthier planet and instill lifelong habits of sustainability in the next generation.

Chapter (20) Culinary Adventures

A. Exploring Different Cultures Through Food:

- Introduce children to diverse cuisines from around the world by exploring foods from different countries and regions.
- Use mealtime as an opportunity to learn about cultural traditions, culinary techniques, and unique ingredients from various cultures.

B. Learning About Global Cuisines with Authentic Recipes:

- Cook authentic recipes from different cultures together as a family, using traditional ingredients and cooking methods to experience the flavors of other countries.
- Research the history and cultural significance of each dish to deepen understanding and appreciation for the culinary heritage of diverse communities.

C. Encouraging Cultural Appreciation and Diversity:

- Foster an environment of cultural appreciation and respect by celebrating the richness and diversity of global cuisines.
- Encourage children to ask questions, share their own cultural traditions, and learn from others with different backgrounds and experiences.

D. Incorporating Food Traditions from Around the World:

- Incorporate food traditions from around the world into family meals and celebrations to broaden children's cultural experiences and culinary horizons.
- Explore holiday traditions, festivals, and rituals that revolve around food in different cultures, and incorporate them into

your own family traditions.

E. Broadening Children's Palates with Exotic Flavors and Ingredients:

- Introduce children to new and exotic flavors by incorporating spices, herbs, and ingredients from different cuisines into everyday meals.
- Encourage children to try new foods and flavors, and celebrate their willingness to explore and appreciate diverse culinary experiences.

By embarking on culinary adventures that celebrate cultural diversity, you can inspire children to develop a deeper appreciation for global cuisines, broaden their palates, and foster a sense of curiosity and respect for the world around them.

❖ Conclusion

A. Recap of the Importance of Creative and Nutritious Lunches:

- Creative and nutritious lunches are essential for children's growth, development, and overall well-being.
- Providing balanced meals packed with a variety of nutrients ensures that children have the energy and focus they need to thrive throughout the day.
- Incorporating creativity into lunch box packing makes mealtime enjoyable and exciting for children, encouraging them to develop healthy eating habits that will last a lifetime.

B. Encouragement for Experimenting and Trying New Recipes:

- Experimenting with new recipes and ingredients is a fun and rewarding way to discover delicious and nutritious meal options for children.
- Don't be afraid to step outside of your comfort zone and try new flavors, cuisines, and cooking techniques to keep lunchtime interesting and enjoyable.
- Embrace the opportunity to involve children in the cooking process, fostering their curiosity and creativity in the kitchen while teaching them valuable life skills.

C. Happy Lunch Box Packing!

- As you embark on your lunch box packing journey, remember to prioritize balance, variety, and creativity in your meal planning.
- With a little preparation and creativity, you can create delicious, nutritious, and exciting lunches that your children will love.

Enjoy the process of packing lunch boxes, knowing that you're providing your children with the fuel they need to thrive and succeed each day.

www.ingramcontent.com/pod-product-compliance
Lightning Source LLC
Chambersburg PA
CBHW020650160726
47991CB00003B/1116